This book belongs to

....

This is the story of Coralie,

a mermaid princess, living under the sea.

There's something else in this story, as well –

on every page, can you spot the seashell?

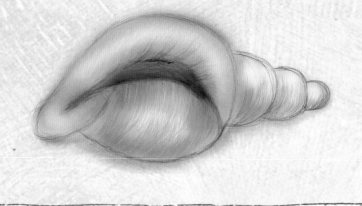

The Little Mermaid

Nick and Claire Page

Illustrations by Katie Saunders

make
believe
ideas

In a beautiful palace,
under the sea,
lived a mermaid princess
who was called Coralie.
As she played with the gulls,
one grey, windy dawn,
she saw a small boat
that was caught in a storm.

Prince Roderick was fishing
for pearls in the sea,
when a wave hit the boat!
He fell in, "Quick! Help me!"
She rescued the prince,
brought him safe to the bay,
sang softly to wake him
and then swam away.

Back at the palace, her head's in a whirl,
"I wish – how I wish – that I was a girl!"
Her sisters, called Laura and Flora and Dora,
said, "Why don't you go to see Seaweedy Nora?

Now Nora was smelly and not very nice.
She liked to eat jellyfish, sea-slugs and lice.

At the back of her cave,
deep down in the ocean,
Seaweedy Nora
mixed up a dark potion.

Nora said, "Here, I can give you your wish.
Drink this and you'll be a lot less like a fish.
Now pay me by filling this shell with your voice!
So Coralie paid — there was simply no choice.

She drank up the drink
(it smelled of fish eggs)
and when she reached land,
her tail became legs!

Later, Prince Roderick sailed past her once more and said to her, "Haven't I seen you before?"

But she couldn't speak,
so looked into his eyes.
She stepped into the boat,
and to her surprise,
the prince leaned towards her,
to give her a kiss.
But Seaweedy Nora said,
"I must stop this!"

With Coralie's voice, she sang,
"Prince, come to me!"
and the prince, now enchanted,
jumped into the sea!

Coralie watched but could not say a word.
Then, on a rock near her, she spotted a bird.

The bird went and fetched
all of Coralie's friends –
seagulls and crabs,
and a lobster called Ben.
They pecked at old Nora
and broke the seashell.
Coralie's voice was released –
they had broken the spell!

Seaweedy Nora was chased far away,
and the prince and the mermaid
were married that day.
Now the mermaid's a girl,
Coralie has her wish –
but sometimes she wishes
that she was a fish!

Ready to tell

Oh no! Some of the pictures from this story have been mixed up! Can you retell the story and point to each picture in the correct order?

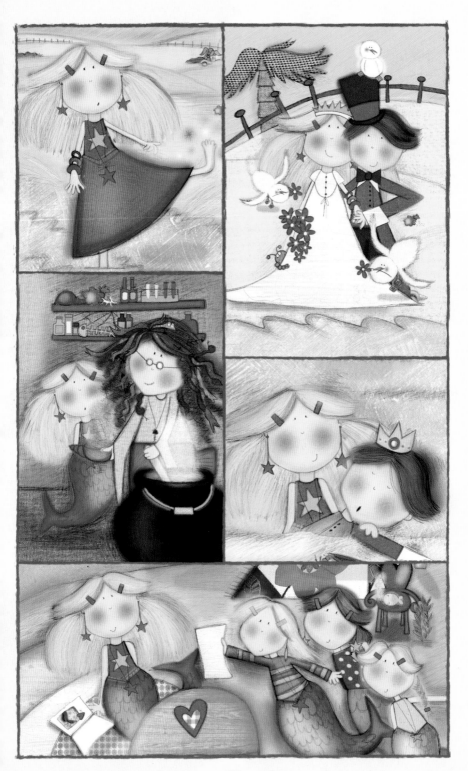

Picture dictionary

Encourage your child to read these words from the story and gradually develop his or her basic vocabulary.

birds

boat

girl

legs

mermaids

prince

sea

shell

swim

Key words

Here are some key words used in context. Help your child to use other words from the border in simple sentences.

Coralie **is** a mermaid.

She saves Prince Peter.

Coralie **goes** to see Seaweedy Nora.

Coralie **sees** the boat.

The prince and Coralie **are** very happy.

Make a starfish necklace

Would you like to be a mermaid? Why not put on a bikini top, wrap your legs in shiny material, and make this beautiful starfish necklace?

You will need

white glue . a toothpick . waxed paper . sand or glitter . a paper clip . narrow ribbon or cord

What to do

1 Carefully squeeze some glue onto the waxed paper, in the shape of a small starfish. Use the toothpick to help shape the glue.

2 Ask an adult to bend a paper clip into a "V" shape.

3 Put the ends of a paper clip into the glue at the end of one arm of the starfish.

4 Sprinkle the glue lightly with sand or glitter.

5 Gently shake off the excess sand or glitter.

6 Let it dry completely. (This will take all night and sometimes longer.)

7 Carefully peel the waxed paper off the back of the starfish.

8 Thread about 1½ feet (½ meter) of narrow ribbon, or other cord, through the paper clip. Tie it in a knot.

Slip the necklace over your head and sing like a mermaid!